Successful Leaders' Secrets
to Survive in Business

Successful Leaders' Secrets to Survive in Business

◆

A "Thinkbook"

Roger G. Lewandowski

iUniverse, Inc.
New York Lincoln Shanghai

Successful Leaders' Secrets to Survive in Business
A "Thinkbook"

iUniverse books may be ordered through booksellers or by contacting:

iUniverse
2021 Pine Lake Road, Suite 100
Lincoln, NE 68512
www.iuniverse.com
1-800-Authors (1-800-288-4677)

ISBN: 978-0-595-43425-1 (pbk)
ISBN: 978-0-595-87749-2 (ebk)

Printed in the United States of America

This book is dedicated to Norma Jean Lewandowski, whose support, patience and sacrifice over all the years have been indispensable, whom I treasure not only as a wife and as mother of my children, *but also as my best friend.*

Contents

PREFACE

There was a time when people who held executive positions had job security for a lifetime and they would have had to do something rather drastic to be fired.

The number of turnovers in executive positions is shocking in today's world. Society accepts this as a common occurrence. (The average tenure for a CEO today is only three years.)

Executives are "discharged" or officially announced as "leaving for personal reasons," but the bottom line is that they still lose their positions. Patience and loyalty seem to be things of the past, and downsizing and outsourcing worldwide are compounding the problem of security for executives. The answer for security in any position is to make sure the business *needs you* more than you need them.

I have written this book to give you ideas about where to excel, sharing with you secrets you might have forgotten and giving you new ones to which you have never been exposed. They are deceptively simple and neither Harvard nor Yale teaches them, yet they are time-tested secrets that work.

I ask you to keep on open mind as you read this book and ask yourself where you could use these ideas. Brainstorm and write them down with target dates. Even though I mention these two key points again in the book, I want to highlight them here:

1. **It is not that executives do not know what to do that causes a crisis—it is their failure to take timely action.**

2. **The most overlooked and under-utilized tool management has is to follow through *with a passion* in the implementation of their plans. If you show your passion for success, it will be contagious to all your people. If you fail to do so, your people will see this as "just another project of the month."**

I believe American industry can win against anyone if businesses do their homework properly, utilize their people's talents, and implement quickly in this worldwide war of business.

Roger G. Lewandowski

P.S. *Read this book very carefully!* There is at least *one idea* that may save your job or can ensure your promotion and success if acted on quickly!

This is no ordinary book to read, it is a "thinkbook" with space for your ideas or action plans to consider and explore.

INTRODUCTION

Unlike business concepts or philosophies with an overall theme, this book contains information on individual business "secrets" that can stand alone. You and your general management team will be able to use these ideas throughout various areas of your business.

My main purpose is to plant seeds for your consideration in your unique product, marketplace, and organization.

I would suggest you use this book as a "**thinkbook**" and go back and read it monthly. **Change what I suggested, perhaps, into a better idea. Make notes so you will not forget your thoughts or action plans. Good luck and good hunting!**

YOU!

Today's world is becoming more demanding on leaders whether they are football coaches, politicians, or management executives. People expect them to win every day, and there is less and less tolerance for failure.

The higher the executive's position, the more his/her stockholders, customers and employees expect his/her performance to be perfect. The executive cannot have (or show) the "normal" weaknesses of an average person. Because of this, leaders tend to be true egotists who are always at the edge. However, the reward is what they seek. Like the reincarnated Attila the Hun, Alexander the Great, or Patton, these leaders love the thrill of victory and the thrill of the battle itself.

It is sad to say, but nice people *do not* finish first in war or business regardless of how public relations people paint them. In the inner sanctum, the real winners are known for what they are—fanatical to get the job done.

These people (the fanatics), who have the best of intentions, must recognize that they are sacrificing time: time with their family and time for a normal relationship with a wife or husband, children, relatives, etc. Unfortunately, they will also find they are not immortal.

Do you fit one of these descriptions: a nice person who is trying to play it straight or a fanatic who wants to win at all costs? The one common thing between these two types of people (and you too will be affected by it) is that they will discover that business is a very demanding mistress/lover. The more time spent with him/her, the more time he/she will demand. He/she is not very forgiving either, so you must be very careful about your priorities.

Secret: Great leaders are great actors who know how to play the right part when needed and avoid making enemies in business. The really big secret only you can answer is—What do you want to do with the rest of your life?

Notes or Action Plans:

_____

_____

_____

BIG IS BAD, SMALL IS GOOD, AND CASH FLOW IS KING!

This is probably the most important secret you must recognize. Because of its importance, I devote more effort to each category, clarifying what I mean when I say that **big is bad, small is good, and cash flow is king.**

I do not know the size of your operation. Regardless, if you are a corporate president, a small supplier, or a service organization, your building is probably too big for your business to work efficiently. In addition, you may also have too many employees to run it efficiently and you may be in real danger of not surviving.

Simply downsizing or outsourcing your work may not be the answer, although it is the current trend. The real answer is a total strategy that is phased-in properly and changes the way you do business. There are no substitutes, and band-aids will only prolong the inevitable. You must face reality and ask yourself, "What business am I in?"

Perhaps I should say, "time out," and give you a summary of why I feel *big is bad*. The following points play important parts in your evaluation:

BIG IS BAD

It is easier to manage a small organization than a large one; therefore, regardless of your size, you should look at restructuring yourself. The way to do that, once you identify what product or service you wish to perform exceptionally well, is to incorporate an old-fashioned concept called "zero-based budgeting." This concept starts with a clean sheet of paper, and for every expenditure or person that you put onto your organization sheet or budget, ask yourself, "Why? How can I eliminate this need or function? Can I outsource this skill and use it only as needed? Do I really need to pay taxes on this large building, pay environmental costs and pay high-energy costs? Should I lease, not own property, to be more flexible to move as required?"

The people that you employ are the key to your organization; but, today it is difficult (and tomorrow will be even more difficult) to find good people you can trust. You want people who have the enthusiasm you have, who have the basic skills required to accomplish your set objectives.

The people that you do bring on board will demand more and more fringe benefits, particularly as the cost of everything rises in the next few years—the leading cost will be health care and medical costs. The cost of doing business will become more and more exorbitant and the performance of those in business may decline.

If you are hesitant in considering outsourcing, remember, Wal-Mart, Sears, and Nike are just a few of the winners who do not manufacture anything they sell. General Electric now makes approximately 40 percent of its profits from the *services* they perform.

I believe that there will be a huge impact in the next five years on the business outsourced overseas. This will be caused by those countries growing impatient to have the good life. The politics of these countries, mainly China, India, and Russia, will have to respond by taking away a lot of the exporting capacity from factories and redirect it internally for their citizens in order to avoid uprisings. This will leave U.S. outsourced factories in a dangerous condition because they will become second priority for the products built in those countries, and our factories will not be tooled to have the technology needed to get back in the competition.

Therefore, you must start with a clean sheet of paper. Once you determine your type of business, you have to *do it differently* than anyone else is doing it today. *You must lead.* You *cannot* be a follower because in our rapidly expanding world economy of today, you must compete with labor markets in China, India and other countries in everything you do.

SMALL IS GOOD

Obviously, the opposite of all the things I said above helps substantiate why I say that small is good. Smaller-scale businesses allow for lower cost for taxes, people, and facilities. I expect corporations will continue to rethink what their core processes are and not produce all they do today. They may assemble only; they will outsource salary functions also.

Nevertheless, if you accept that "small is good" as a possibility, and there is not a roadmap for you to follow, where should you look? Let me share a few ideas with you.

You should move your location "every ten years" (lease). This will help reduce retirement and health care cost because of a younger work force. You may not be able to do it instantaneously, but change your location. There are only three secrets to retail: location, location and location—it is also true in any business. Look at your business, perhaps not for today but in the near future.

You should consider moving to a rural area or to a state whose management would be willing to pay more and give you free taxes. This gives you a fresh start on an organization where you take along with you only those key people who possess necessary skills and those who can contribute to your profitability.

CASH FLOW IS KING

More businesses have gone under, not because of their product or service, their poor quality, or their unacceptable delivery, but because they have not controlled their cash flow. They allowed their inventory to get out of control, they neglected to expedite, and they were too lenient about their accounts receivable. There is nothing in any business more important than cash flow. Cash flow is the gasoline that runs your business engine.

One of the ways to control cash flow is to ask the question "What will this expenditure do to increase the profitability of the business and how long will it take to see the return because of this action."

If the answer is that it will not contribute to the business but will be convenient, ego satisfying, or for appearances only, you do not spend the money. You cannot cash any of those things at the bank.

The discipline of not spending money unless you make money is extremely difficult to sustain, particularly as you begin making money. That is a very critical time in a business because you can move backwards financially faster than you can move forward.

Simply said, *cash flow is king* is good common sense. The courts are full of people who started to make good money, conditions changed and they went bankrupt. In fact, bankruptcies have risen at an alarming rate. It is just another indicator that you can do everything else right, but if you don't control your cash flow, then you are in trouble. Cash flow will always be critical regardless the size of your business.

Notes or Action Plans:

_____

_____

_____

THE FUTURE IN MARKETING IS INDIVIDUAL CUSTOMIZATION OF PRODUCT

The future in marketing is already at hand. There are still many companies and corporations struggling to maintain a standardization of products with the majority of the volume being their *normal, standard* products (a commodity). The world is already changing—people want more variety these days.

You have but to walk into the local supermarket and try to make a decision on what type of bread you should purchase. There are many varieties of health bread and many varieties of healthy bread. Should you have wheat, whole grain, or white? It is not a simple decision. Even as you walk down the aisle toward simple things like milk (simple in the old days), you have many different variations: different percentages of fat, skim milk, even artificial milk. Proceed down the aisle to the potato chips and notice the variety in any given store! In one store, I took a count recently. There were thirty-five different varieties of potato chips ranging from the classic plain to Mexican, Italian, etc. Increases in choices and variation have jaded today's consumers and now they want something different—something special. This is true in all aspects of their lives and for those who want to get the market share, they must accept this fact.

These customized products have a premium price, if you notice, which means a premium in profit. For those trying to sell a so-called "standard" item, they lose not only potential volume, but they lose profit because their margins are smaller and because their price is lower in those markets.

Therefore, you must do what you can to disguise the standardization in your products—a few thoughts:

1. In the process used to manufacture or make a product (i.e., metal, clothing, or food), the basic machinery, or ingredients required should be the same as much as possible. There you have standardization.

2. If you are manufacturing a product, try to have a standard base *hidden in your design or platform*, and then your differences are in elaborate accessories or added components that change the outward appearance. The internal core should essentially be the same. This is where you hide your standardization.

3. You must try to meet the special needs of all your customers. In the designing of whatever you build or make, it should be made uniquely different from the competition. Those who have enough imagination to discover new areas to feed the desires for something new or different will sell, particularly if you are the originator of this new product or process. Remember, with today's technology, you can address reverse engineering as an alternate action.

Notes or Action Plans:

PRETEND SOMEONE JUST FIRED YOU.
NOW YOU ARE THE NEW PERSON IN THE POSITION.

WHAT WILL YOU DO DIFFERENTLY?

The simple experiment, if taken with positive self-analysis, can be one of the most powerful things that you have done for yourself and your organization in some time.

You must come into your office on a given Monday morning and pretend that your old self was fired, even if you are the owner. You have been replaced. You must accept this mental thought, sit down at your desk, and evaluate the paper, programs, and priorities. You do this from a fresh point of view, a clean sheet of paper if you will.

You must ask yourself, "If I am now this new person taking over, what will I do differently? What are the priorities, realistically, to the times? Have they grown into habit? Have I allowed expenses to increase? Is there a bit of lethargy in the organization? Have I allowed my business plan to be less disciplined, and am I really acting on what happens today rather than what I want to happen for tomorrow?"

This should not be taken lightly. Take every item and re-evaluate it with new meaning and new direction. The result of an in-depth review is that you can kick-start or re-energize your organization and become not only more profitable, but also you can put more fun into the work.

Notes or Action Plans:

_____

_____

_____

_____

_____

_____

_____

_____

_____

_____

_____

_____

_____

_____

_____

_____

_____

_____

_____

_____

_____

_____

_____

_____

_____

_____

_____

_____

NEVER TRY TO IMPROVE AN OBSOLETE PROCESS OR STRATEGY

It is a weakness in the human spirit to be reluctant to admit failure. People will continue to chase an objective, a process, or strategy that is no longer viable and is actually obsolete. People spend days, months, and large amounts of money and even offer miscommunication to an entire organization using an obsolete strategy or process and trying to make it efficient. It is difficult for a leader to say, "I was wrong."

The life curve of technology is being revolutionized every two years. Examples include the evolution of mainframe computers, large calculators becoming handheld calculators, laptop computers, and new and improved software. Soon, the information highway will have us use cell phones and our televisions as new information platforms in all we do. Therefore, you must be competitive, yet very careful in your design, so that you do not design into your product or process too much fixed capital costs that will not be flexible enough for a new product or process and will potentially be obsolete. This could cause you to spend capital monies needlessly and create problems with cash flow among other things. The same is true for an absolute objective or strategy. Do not resist change; embrace it!

Be the first to implement new ideas and processes, and your customers will take pride in being a part of your team. Be last, and you will soon be out of business.

Notes or Action Plans:

_____

_____

_____

_____

_____

PRETEND YOUR PRESENT DISTRIBUTION WILL BE TERMINAL IN SIX MONTHS.

HOW WOULD YOU GO TO MARKET NOW?

The distribution taking place today in your organization needs a complete and honest analysis. The world itself is becoming smaller; products from countries unheard of in the past appear in the market more and more with excellent quality and very competitive prices.

In the past, distances of time and space (across the oceans), and technology have protected the United States. Now, however, distance is no longer a barrier due to rapid transportation, rapid distribution of information and exper-tise—people constantly share new technologies throughout the world.

Those monuments of distribution formed in the United States in the past are collapsing or being bypassed by new methods of entering the marketplace. This is particularly true as more and more homemakers work. Not only the husbands, but the women, too, are working and unavailable during the daytime. In the eve-nings, because of their working schedules, they are too tired to go out shopping as they have done in the past. You can already see the start of an avalanche of mail order and do-it-yourself books for every conceivable item used in the home. Store traffic in general will be less accepted for the very large businesses like Wal-Mart, who I predict will offer all kinds of "social magnets" such as concerts, drawings, and contests to become a social center to avoid boredom or loneliness. New ways of distributing will take place and old ones reinvented.

As the information highway expands, you will be able to order merchandise and services from the television. The point is that you must look at your total distribution efforts today and its cost. Pretend it was burned or disposed of. How would you take a fresh look at now serving your ultimate customers/consumers or even distribute to them differently than your practices today?

Notes or Action Plans:

_____
_____
_____
_____
_____
_____
_____
_____
_____
_____
_____
_____
_____
_____
_____
_____
_____
_____
_____
_____
_____
_____
_____
_____
_____
_____
_____
_____
_____
_____
_____

QUALITY IS NOT FREE, BUT IT'S AN "UNMINED" GOLDMINE

Philip B. Crosby wrote a book called *Quality Is Free*, but lately, management is finding out that it is not very true. There is a price for the efforts to sustain quality and to maintain all the statistics to manage it.

There is a treasure chest of gold to be found in every organization because most organizations do not know the true costs of quality. These costs not only include warranties and lost sales, but also inefficiencies, duplications, scrap, rework, overtime, special transportation costs or shipments to the customer, etc. The list can get quite lengthy, but you need to assess it to know what your cost really is. You will see that you probably have a better opportunity to save money on quality than you have to increase your price in the marketplace.

Even though you would make more money by improving quality, there is a danger that you would begin to attack it in a traditional sense—into large statistical analysis, charting of fragment parts in the shop or offices. The better option is simply to accelerate the normal things that you do with more disciplined, measured results. This will generate a huge amount of dollars, but it will also cost dollars, and you must be careful as to how you spend the money. Use common sense.

The real answer is to design the product so that it is unable to be assembled or unable to leave your facility unless it is an excellent, quality product. It would be foolish to spend extravagant amounts of money on testing at the end of the assembly line. The product design itself should be as totally foolproof as possible and the manufacturing process should have its own checkpoints at every step, so that it is impossible to go to the next step of operation until the prior operation is done successfully. This is the real answer to saving money on quality. Pursue this as quickly as possible—and while temporarily taking this approach on your standard-type items that you just *began* to improve, expect all parts internally or from outside suppliers to meet the same quality standards. Truly, the zero-based defects take place at the very start, not at the end of the assembly line—*prevention.*

Last, but not least (in the untapped goldmine) is the office area. I believe managers hesitate to address the office area either because it is "too close to home," (that is, they know all the people too personally, and they want to be loved as leaders) or because doing away with office positions may remove their defense barriers. They would have to be more involved and accountable. In addition, they will not be able to delegate the uncomfortable decisions to others. They key question is, "Why aren't you addressing the office area?" You must consider outsourcing (locally, or within the country), zero-based budgeting, and other opportunities that help to control costs in the office area, such as mapping the process and eliminating all duplication or waste.

Notes or Action Plans:

STAY CLOSE!
OPEN MINI-PROFIT
CENTERS NEAR YOUR
CUSTOMERS

In today's quest for speed and cash flow, it is important that little time be lost in transportation. In your own case, it will cost you more money to buy your staples, when you forget them, at a small food outlet than to go to a supermarket that is much farther away. You will be paying a premium for the things that you buy rather than make the extra time for this trip and the loss of precious time. The same thing is true for your customers. If you can locate as close as you can to your major customers, you will be successful over your competition. An example of this is Wal-Mart and the explosion that they have had as they have located to the rural areas closer to their consumers.

In researching relocation, you should look at breaking up the size of your present business and make mini profit centers close to your major customers. You will have the advantage of being closer to the customers and have control that is more exact. In the process of moving, use caution not to duplicate the service/support areas. You should keep a small, centralized support group that will service the mini profit centers.

You should also check with the local or state governments and ask for their assistance in procuring land or buildings, training, deferring taxes and any other special advantages that you can think of that would maximize your profits by relocating to a given state or community. Do not forget, all states will respond in today's economy for additional jobs, so you must marry the capabilities to be close to your customer and secure the best advantage in the process from the state and local governments.

Another advantage to relocating is that it forces you to re-think your business. Not only with the mini profit centers, but also as to the caliber of people you want to transfer with you, how large the organization will be and how the organization will operate. To move to another area without first making an analysis is making a mistake, losing a tremendous opportunity—and possibly your business.

Notes or Action Plans:

_____

_____

_____

_____

_____

_____

_____

_____

_____

_____

_____

_____

_____

_____

_____

_____

_____

_____

_____

_____

_____

_____

_____

_____

_____

_____

_____

_____

_____

_____

_____

COMPLIMENTS ARE LIKE FLIRTATIONS:

TO BE ENJOYED, BUT NOT TAKEN SERIOUSLY

How many times have you seen people who were complimented about achieving some objective in business, and within a very short time, they have either fallen out of grace or been demoted, fired or encouraged to leave the organization?

Everyone appreciates being successful and recognized for success and contributions. The good leadership of companies and organizations make sure that if they are anything, they are overgenerous in the compliments when people have earned them. You, as an individual, must enjoy the moment in the sun but not become complacent. ***Strive to achieve even greater success*** because success comes not only with compliments but also with security, satisfaction and all the things that go with it financially.

Leadership is truly a lonely position. You cannot always be yourself, but must be what people expect of you.

Notes or Action Plans:

_____
_____
_____
_____
_____
_____
_____
_____
_____
_____

GIVE A CASH REWARD TO UNIVERSITIES THAT CAN MEET OR EXCEED YOUR DESIGN SPECIFICATIONS

As tremendous change in technologies explode across all segments of the economy, it is difficult to be at the edge of the envelope of all new ideas and approaches. There is also a danger that the familiarity of what has been done in the past becomes accepted by everyone that comes along in the future. New designers may only create minor variations to the product's so-called, "previously successful" design.

I believe that there is a unique and very economical way to avoid the additional cost of research and development, which can be used either directly or indirectly as a supplement to the current process. Contact your best universities or colleges, *large or small*, which have the engineering requirements that fit your product or process needs. Present this challenge to the university president: if the university's engineering students create a successful design, the engineering department of the university will receive a cash reward. In addition, the students that excel in this area will receive something that they can legally accept and will become prime candidates to join your company or organization.

You might even take your challenge to two or three universities and have a competition between them where you judge the prototypes on an agreed date for a resolution as to the winner. This would add more excitement and pride for the students; and from your standpoint, you would have three teams working on the project rather than one. It does not necessarily have to be a large university. A smaller university that is less bureaucratic and more flexible in its thinking can accomplish many great things, and will be more of a personal team member.

If you think back on many of the large corporations today, they started up with a new idea in either garages or basements. Therefore, it is reasonable to think that given the right education of the students, the right facilities, support and challenge, you could kick-start a unique breakthrough for your segment of the marketplace. Many times, big things evolve from very small beginnings.

Notes or Action Plans:

_____
_____
_____
_____
_____
_____
_____
_____
_____
_____
_____
_____
_____
_____
_____
_____
_____
_____
_____
_____
_____
_____
_____
_____
_____

MOMENTUM IN BUSINESS

You must redirect your thinking in business measurements so that you relate everything to cost. Many measurements of the past are obsolete, and it is a waste of time and money to use them. Examples might include such measurements as direct-to-indirect ratios, plant absorption, and salary-to-hourly ratios.

You must concentrate on dollars so that everyone can relate to making money—which is the reason you are in business. Therefore, you should examine all items, not as a solution or silver bullet, but as indicators that relate to sales dollars. In other words, what are your big expenses in advertising per sales dollars? What are your research dollars as a percentage of sales dollars? What are your manufacturing costs as a percentage of sales dollars? What are the trend lines?

You must continually look at reducing product cost each year. It does not matter what the total manufacturing expense is, even as it relates to percentage of sales (which is just an *indicator*, as I said earlier). The true measure of manufacturing begins with, "What does this product cost?" This should be continually going down each year. I am not talking about labor costs only; I am talking about the design material costs that are normally the majority of the cost of the product.

The measurement of the product cost itself is not a violation of my point to measure dollars as a ratio to sales. In order to be competitive, you should always compare your product costs to what it has been so that your pricing (which is independent of product cost and controlled by the marketplace) can be competitive to generate additional business.

As I indicated, all costs should be value added to making money. One basic principle I apply at all times is, "The momentum should always be for improvement off a base." Your base may not be accurate for whatever reason, but at least if you have a base, you can measure your performance for now and for the future. You want to reduce it continuously. *Always* **spend less time on determining the base, but always watch the trend lines so that they are moving in the *right direction* and in a *timely manner*. This will avoid complacency.**

Notes or Action Plans:

_____
_____
_____
_____
_____
_____
_____
_____
_____
_____
_____
_____
_____
_____
_____
_____
_____
_____
_____
_____
_____
_____
_____
_____
_____
_____
_____
_____
_____
_____

WHEN IN DOUBT, USE THE "DO NOTHING" POLICY

It is not a contradiction to say that you want momentum to press the attack, yet at the same time hesitate to make certain decisions.

It is dangerous as an executive to feel infallible or to make decisions quickly on any given subject. There is then a real risk that major decisions could be made incorrectly.

You must make decisions as if you have manual transmission (five-speed shift) in a car. There are certain simple decisions that you should make quickly and move on. As the decisions become more difficult, you shift down to a lower gear and ask for more information, more input, and more opinions as each decision is made. You must not feel obliged to act hastily with each difficult decision. If in doubt, a very old-fashioned but powerful tool is the "do nothing" policy. It is a fact of life that there are many things that will resolve themselves if given time and left alone. This is particularly true when you have fears about any subject (business or personal)—you are likely to overreact, and it may be better to wait. It is better that you have confidence and faith in yourself and do nothing until you have more facts, or the situation becomes more obvious as to which options are best.

It is an uncomfortable truth, though, that in today's industry, there are many executives who feel obliged to make all decisions on everything, and make them *now*. It can be fatal for your organization and your career. Only the foolish rush into making decisions; make timely decisions, but with deliberate speed as needed.

Notes or Action Plans:

_____

_____

_____

_____

THE ULTIMATE WARRIOR IS A BENEVOLENT DICTATOR

The ultimate warrior in business is a benevolent dictator. It is important to recognize that human beings all want to be loved, understood, and appreciated by everyone. There is no exception; whether you are the president of a company or an hourly worker, all people have basic needs.

In business, there is pressure to make money, and there are conditions that presidents inherit. It is very difficult comfortably being "just one of the team." In fact, it is very rare that presidents can come into a company, become a member of a "team," and make things happen. The very fact that they are "presidents" is an indication that the buck stops with them and that they must make the hard decisions that are not popular. If presidents begin to compromise making those hard decisions, they face the possibility of failure, which influences all employees and customers negatively.

Of course, at the opposite end of the spectrum are the egotists who come in to take over (or are promoted from within) and begin to think they are gods on Earth. They want done whatever they say without question and expect people to treat them with the ultimate respect and homage.

Ultimate warriors are a very rare breed. They know what needs to be done. They will listen to their subordinates, but will decide what the risks are and take the corrective action necessary at the bottom-line time. Contrary to the egotists who want all the glory for themselves, benevolent dictators will share the rewards of victory. They do not have to be like Attila the Hun, who was certainly a benevolent dictator, in that he promised his troops the spoils of the campaign. These warriors, in modern day society, are people who care about their people. They are kind, nurturing types who are stern as parents when necessary but also compassionate for others' needs.

It is difficult to find this type of leader. You have to find people who have the ability and capability to make things happen for the success and security of the employees and the customer. They also must not let success go to their head to the point where they become egotistical or self-centered, which is the shortcoming of many of our leaders. If you search out the top five hundred corporations beneath the public relations image, you will see that there are certain benevolent dictators who are running corporations. I believe, for example, that Iacocca was one who really did care about his people, but he made no mistake when the hard decisions were to be made; he would make them and expect them to be carried out. Currently, I believe that Bill Gates is this type of rare leader as well.

In world competition, you can see much more of this being true, particularly with the Japanese. The Japanese are thought to be team players. If you research their management style, you will find that they will investigate and study things; but at some point, the presidents make decisions and expect completion. In turn, they will take care of their people. Therefore, in Twenty-First Century economy, those who are truly successful and gifted, with the ability to control their egos, will be the ultimate warriors—**these are the benevolent dictators.**

Notes or Action Plans:

_____
_____
_____
_____
_____
_____
_____
_____
_____
_____
_____
_____
_____
_____
_____
_____
_____
_____
_____

TIME IS THE
ULTIMATE WEAPON

Time is the most precious commodity. It is also the most fleeting. It makes no distinction between those who are poor and those who are rich—those who are happy and those who are unhappy. Time moves on and disappears, never to return.

In the daily hustle and bustle of life, people sometimes forget and do not realize the speed at which time is moving past them. This casual attitude about time and its disappearance is also spilling over into the business world.

In the business world, particularly, timing is critical. I believe that timing is everything in business. In today's world, people have the super information highway network and the ability to get data quickly. Many executives do not recognize that they have the weapon of *time* at their disposal. Effective use of time can make executives superior to their competition and more desirable to their customers. One example I can point out and you can relate to is Domino's Pizza. Who would have thought that there was any real money in the pizza business? Pizza Hut had most of the market and most cities already had their own local pizza restaurant. The Domino Corporation recognized that delivery time (generally thirty minutes) could be a competitive weapon. Look what happened after that was discovered and used. Other pizza delivery companies tried to copy them, but it was already too late. Domino's was the first to exploit the weapon of time, and established the trademark of Domino's Pizza as a force with which to be dealt.

We are also seeing a fleeting glance of this in Federal Express. Who would have thought people would pay extra money to receive their mail faster? Once Federal Express was able to institute this, everyone tried to copy them, but it was too late; they too had established themselves as a force. Today, they continue to expand their capabilities and flexibility on this one powerful strategy—***time***.

In running your business, you do not actually have to spend large capital monies to exploit the ultimate weapon of time. It is amazing that, in spite of its simplicity, this is not being done in a more aggressive, assertive manner.

If executives were to look at the time that they use in twenty-four hours, they might find that a majority of the hours are being used inefficiently. They should address this problem and check themselves every day as to how they score on using time and their people's abilities.

Larger corporations in particular, have many conversations and very little action to reduce the time between a product design and its manufacturing. Again, it is done in a bureaucratic type of atmosphere that still makes it a slave to a lengthy time introduction.

I believe that having small teams can circumvent this, like those that initially started large corporations like Xerox, Apple Computer, or E.S.P. Corporation. The list can go on and on of things that were done uniquely different but only done by a few people in a timely manner.

There is an old-fashioned word being used by some corporations—"skunk works." A small group of people are put into an area of design and given the opportunity and the backing to develop products quickly, and left out of the bureaucracy of presentations, updates, meetings, etc.

You will see much more of this taking place with enlightened management in the future. It is difficult to have real breakthroughs when you are working under a bureaucratic type of management. Talent that should be used to develop things is, instead, forced into conformity dictated by bureaucratic types of procedures and perk networks of accomplishments.

Also, time becomes part of the manufacturing process itself. Ninety-five percent of the actual time in a production factory is actually spent in idle, non-value added activities.

The remaining five percent of production time is the time that a screwdriver is driving-in a screw, or that a drill really is creating a hole, not just going back up to its position or indexing. There is a tremendous opportunity in manufacturing beyond lean production and agile manufacturing—to examine manufacturing processes and significantly eliminate non-value added time. One of my tenets is that you must not try to make an obsolete strategy or process work. When implementing lean production—taking a process and making it more efficient—you should dask, "Is the process correct in the first place?" It is a question of time, and of priorities.

Time controls every element of your daily life. It is used in every element of your working life as an executive and as a customer. If you could develop the breakthroughs in time management I mentioned previously, these will give the consumer more time to use in other areas more effectively, and you will increase your share market and be more successful.

The point is that time itself is a valuable commodity. If you can reduce the time in any process, it has huge potential for saving big-time money and increasing the speed to the marketplace.

Warning! A disease that continues to grow is the amount of time spent on poorly organized meetings.

Notes or Action Plans:

_____

_____

_____

_____

_____

_____

_____

_____

_____

_____

_____

_____

_____

_____

_____

_____

_____

_____

_____

_____

_____

_____

_____

_____

_____

_____

_____

ATTACK, ATTACK, ATTACK!

If you study history, you will find many occasions where great victories could have been won if the aggressors had continued to exploit their breakthrough advantage. This might be one of the examples that you can relate to easily. When the Germans broke through France and took over all of Europe in World War II, they procrastinated on invading England. If they had taken over England, who knows what history would be. They might have avoided having a war on two large fronts. Or what would the United States have been like if General Lee persevered and entered Washington (as he approached Washington and saw they had no organized defense) instead of turning back?

More recently in big business, IBM was looked at as "Big Blue" and almost invincible in the computer area. Perhaps because of their large size, the bureaucracy did not allow them to look at the potential they could have in personal computers. Large mainframes were their primary commodity. Consequently, they lost the chance to monopolize this business at the outset. This is also true of General Motors, which at one time was to be broken up because of its enormous size; they were considered a monopoly. What happened was that American management failed to realize the small cars' gas efficiency in the early seventies, and the Japanese just happened to have a vehicle that took advantage of gas shortages and high prices. They took over a large share of the market. Toyota is number two in total sales in the American auto industry today but within five years, it may be number one in the world—not only in the USA.

In response to the question of "attack, attack and attack," you must give the Japanese credit. They have not backed off in pursuit of monopolizing the United States car market. While Congress and/or diplomats play with dialogue year after year about the deficit and importing cars, the Japanese are announcing more expansions of their car manufacturing companies in the United States. In due course, they will solve the deficit problem by having the majority of their cars made in the United States. Then, the problem will be that the profits made from those will just go back to the war chest of the Japanese to exploit other targets of opportunity. The point is that the Japanese have learned the simplicity of "attack, attack and attack."

Today, China is copying the Japanese in attacking the marketplace. The U.S. companies seem to become complacent when they make profitable margins. What they lack is the sense of urgency, and they do not make improvements or revolutionary changes required for their corporations to exploit the markets.

Another aggressive U.S. company (I might call it my *hero*) is Microsoft. In the case of Microsoft, they recognized the right need. While everyone was fighting with mainframes, they saw that the real gasoline running them was software. They were aggressively intelligent enough to do something, and they began to dominate the software area. Today, even though Apple Computers and many others are trying to come back and break the software barrier, Microsoft is progressing to develop more advanced technology. Microsoft's state-of-the-art thinking may go *beyond* the fundamentals of software.

Regardless of size—whether your business is large or small, a parts supplier or a restaurant owner—the common denominator is that you must never rest on your oars. You must be continually looking for improvements and things that will satisfy your customers now as well as in the future. You must be the leaders rather than the followers because the view is not always good for the second horse in a race.

Do you have a real strategic plan or just warmed-up leftovers?

Notes or Action Plans:

_____

_____

_____

_____

_____

_____

_____

_____

_____

_____

_____

_____

_____

_____

_____

_____

THE ULTIMATE
OF PERFECTION
IS SIMPLICITY

If you look at some of the great breakthrough inventions, they are very simple. The problem is that someone else thought of them, not you. They found a need, and they filled it. In today's companies and high-technology world, in the aftermath of the breakthroughs, there are thousands of ideas that can be used to enhance and improve the technologies that are being introduced.

You do not need to expend a tremendous amount of capital on ideas and approaches. It is merely going back to what the Japanese call the "Five Why's." It is, "Why do we do it this way, and why do we need it?" You ask the two questions five times in a row until you get to the core of the need, and then you ask if there is another way of doing it. It is a patient way to make an analysis at an extremely low cost, but it is the genesis of many ideas and many inventions if you just take the time.

In the business world, General Electric has become one of the most progressive, future-oriented corporations in the U.S. I believe that of all the corporations in the U.S. who understand what is needed for the near future and beyond to make money, GE knows it better than anyone does. The only people who come close to understanding GE's approach are some of the larger Japanese corporations.

GE has been slowly but steadily removing themselves from all manufacturing. They do not want to compete with low labor costs around the world. They do not want their capital tied up and not have a return on it. They do not want to be tied down with all the labor problems and benefit costs, particularly with an aging workforce and pension costs.

General Electric sold various low-technology factories and commodities, but they are moving up in their high technologies area. They encourage private branded products to use the GE logo, which has tremendous market value. They are able to exploit this but not have all the headaches of manufacturing.

They are becoming more and more a strategic capital corporation. Strategically, they want to look at the use of capital to make money, not only venture capital, but strategic capital to exploit world opportunities. I believe that under GE's management and leadership, they will continue to excel and lead the rest of the country in this strategic capital use. The only competition they will face will be the Japanese. Who knows? At some point in the future, perhaps they will be joint partners on world opportunities rather than the adversaries.

In other words, you are going to see the same thing that has happened in the past; and as proof, look at Sears of the old days. They made billions and billions of dollars in sales, and they never really had any manufacturing arms. They were conscious enough to recognize the needs of the customers, and they used that vision to establish catalogs in rural and other areas so that they were able to exploit this into success. In more recent years, they forgot their more basic strengths, and were sideswiped by someone who came from ground zero and established the Wal-Mart stores (Sam Walton). And what did Sam Walton do? He went to rural areas rather than to main cities and set up stores that serviced all the needs that the consumer could possibly want as Sears formerly did. Contrary to other large companies with whom they compete, they do have better quality for a better price.

Wal-Mart took away the leadership from Sears by following through on the fundamentals (the simplicities required by the consumers); then, they exploited that by taking the power of their very size today to get the best quality and price. I believe that they will not rest on their laurels, either. They recognize the risks of success and will continue to exploit them. They must be careful not to complicate things from the success that they have had, and to nurture that simplicity to higher potential that is available to them, in the U.S. and throughout the world.

If there is a put-down to the slogan of the "the ultimate of simplicity," it would be believing that hi-tech will solve everything. This idea could be costly to a corporation. The *simplicity strategy* does not mean you should not use every tech tool available; just use it wisely. This idea can be used in every portion of any company or organization. Again, you must look at trying to keep things as simple as possible while taking care of the customer. That would be perfection—not spending money on ego trips and personal satisfaction or building monuments for yourself based on your facilities or living style.

Is your strategy planning too complicated for today's revolution?

Notes or Action Plans:

_____
_____
_____
_____
_____
_____
_____
_____
_____
_____
_____
_____
_____
_____
_____
_____
_____
_____
_____
_____
_____
_____
_____
_____
_____
_____
_____
_____
_____
_____
_____
_____
_____

IF YOU CAN'T MEASURE IT, DON'T DO IT!

Nothing says that you have to be decisive on everything you do. In too many offices, as well as various factories, things are done just because someone said to do them; and no one has addressed what this means in making money. **The key in business is always to make money.**

Before you do *anything* in any area of your business or service industry, you must ask yourself why you are going to do it. The second question is also very important; ask yourself how you will measure its success. If you cannot figure out a way to measure it, do not do it. It will be a waste of money and there is no value added.

As your business becomes more complex, the tendency to do things because someone said so escalates. Regardless of your enterprise, it is like a piece of machinery. It must be oiled so that it will run smoothly. Any object thrown into a piece of machinery will jeopardize its efficiency and eventually the machine will break down. This is true in all aspects of business.

Many people measure the value of things based on reactions, conversations because of a meeting, or someone's interpretation of what the boss wants. This insidious thing takes place when there are no established plans. Workers try to please the boss with what they think he or she would like and do not recognize the consequences if it is not the right thing to do.

Many things are being done that should not be done. In the world of high-tech capabilities that include computers, machinery and automation, it is easy to neglect this *casual but powerful, day-to-day fact*. Even major decisions by management are not always examined with scrutiny *to ensure you can benchmark the success* of what you are attempting to do.

Benchmarking is a simple, hidden opportunity that management of any size operation has at their disposal—with little cost. Think about this. Be honest with yourself and watch what happens in your organization in just one day or week after you *only do* what you can *measure*. You can save millions by changing the culture of decision making.

Notes or Action Plans:

_____

_____

_____

_____

_____

_____

_____

_____

_____

_____

_____

_____

_____

_____

_____

_____

_____

_____

_____

_____

_____

_____

_____

_____

_____

_____

_____

_____

_____

_____

_____

_____

_____

_____

SALESPEOPLE ARE THE KEYS TO FINANCIAL STABILITY. DO YOU HAVE THE RIGHT KEYS?

The slogan, "Nothing happens before a sale is made," from a financial standpoint, is true and generally accepted.

In the hustle and bustle of today's activities, though, the sales area sometimes reaches second or third position as far as using sales personnel and spending time analyzing the way to even the market.

The world has changed dramatically in just the last five years. The number of households where both parents work continues to rise. The amount of money being controlled by the woman of the household continues to climb. Today, women are the dominant source of how money is controlled in the area of cash flow in the U.S. This means that some organizations must rethink the way they go to sales. They cannot go out and perform their function in the routine traditional (male-focused) manner and bureaucratic style of days gone by.

You hear about network marketing. Perhaps this is one approach. Your product is unique in its own way, and you must figure out if your method of distribution is still viable in today's world. More importantly, you must figure out if your product will be viable three or five years from now.

There are meetings held constantly in companies regarding new product designs and computer applications, but there are not enough meetings being held on how to go to market. What breakthroughs can you make differently from your competitors in going to market? Who will the salespeople be, and what will their duties be compared to what they were in the past?

In too many cases today, businesses are "faking it" by using traditional types of sales structures with district sales managers, vice presidents of sales and salespeople. They go through the war dance, if you will, on their sales meetings and then go to outings with the customers and become order takers rather than true salespeople. These are all fine and great if you are the sales representative, but from the standpoint of the company and corporation, what should the sales force be doing differently today? They are your front line to the consumer, and they are the ones that can make or break a corporation in spite of all the technology, elaborate factories, or engineering.

They should be evaluated, trained, and rewarded properly. They should be like troops in combat—expendable if they cannot meet the needs of a corporation, company, or service industry.

Notes or Action Plans:

_____
_____
_____
_____
_____
_____
_____
_____
_____
_____
_____
_____
_____
_____
_____
_____
_____
_____
_____
_____
_____
_____
_____
_____
_____

SALARIED EMPLOYEES (CONTRACT EMPLOYEES)

As business changes into a world economy, it is becoming more and more difficult to know exactly how you stand against your competition. In the past, it was relatively easy to know who your competition was. We saw Japan become a world factor in industry. In today's automotive world, they are gaining more strength and could well be *number one* in as little as five years. Who was thinking ten years ago that China would be competitive today? Where will they be in five years? Korea, India, and Eastern Europe are beginning to be competitors. South America will be the surprise in the next five years.

My point is, committing too much to your salary force in job security and benefits may become dangerous to your profitability and existence. For the future, I see much more outsourcing, use of part-time employees, temporary employees, and retirees working less than thirty hours a week—perhaps from home. Full-time employees will be working on two- or three-year contacts in the future. This means a complete rethinking of job descriptions and *purpose*. It also means that the salaried employees cannot be complacent. The quality of salaried people should be continuously improving, as should the process. Competitors have core manufacturing processes that are critical, and so are the core salary people. Do you know what positions they are?

Notes or Action Plans:

_____
_____
_____
_____
_____
_____
_____
_____

THE *RIGHT* PART-TIME EMPLOYEES ARE *POWERFUL*

In today's economy, businesses have seen the continued use of part-time help on the rise. Businesses of all sizes have recognized that if they use part-time help, they can avoid the expenses of health care and pensions. They can also be moved much easier than "permanent employees" can. You will see this even in large corporations, such as in the car industry, which uses part-time help extensively (even in the salaried ranks) and the fast food industry where the use of part-time employees is almost the norm.

As the trend grows in the future, you will see for the first time ever, contract employees and salaried people hired at low levels—not only as presidents. They will get one, two, or three-year contracts. I predict this will be the new rage because it gives management a chance to be more flexible. The public has a negative perception of "downsizing" because of the way it's being done today. Hiring contract employees will help businesses to have a more comfortable reduction of head count and to become more flexible. **The future of downsizing will be contract, salary employees.**

I believe that the new wave in hourly, part-time employees will be the use of homemakers and retired people with many skills. There is nothing magic about an eight-hour day, and you are hearing more and more about flextime. Many homemakers can come in and work for four hours after the children have gone to school, and leave in time to pick them up. These working parents will be contributing more to society; and from a financial standpoint, they will not have the cost of day-care centers to diminish their paychecks.

Parents of small children also could have the opportunity to work second shift. They could be home, caring for preschool-age children all day, and when their spouse comes home at night, go and work four hours in the evenings. They would be contributing four hours of skilled, high-caliber work from an excellent workforce that has not been tapped. With so much downsizing occurring today, industries (of any size) should be utilizing the special skills of retirees.

I believe management should tap into these resources in an organized fashion—as in all aspects of business. I believe what should be done (this is simple and costs little) is to utilize local people near your factory—so that travel is not a real problem—and bring in these people as "sidewalk alumni." Business leaders should recruit, train, and retain them (on standby) for seasonal upswings. They would be available when the need for special programs arise, or for vacation relief for employees. These people would be brought in as a kind of team, if you will, into an "auditorium." Management would lecture these people about the culture of that organization and provide a special newsletter for them. They would receive certain distinctions: a hat, t-shirt or some other type of apparel, so they would have a certain pride in being a part of the alumni.

Take the time to train these people properly and spend the personal time with them—such as having a cup of coffee and doughnuts, giving them factory tours and monthly training sessions. It would be like a social club to them, in a sense, and you would have a highly-skilled, talented workforce—that I predict, in many cases, would be more efficient and more trustworthy than the ones you have today (who have basically a ho-hum attitude).

Instead of using trained intellectuals (in the salaried ranks) to assist on special programs, vacations, particular business or new ventures, you would be surprised what a pool of knowledge the *right part-time employees* may bring to your workplace. Because they are new, they want to prove themselves. Because they are retired, they want to prove that they have value. All these things can complement an elite workforce available to you at an extremely low cost. Why do companies and corporations not exploit this today? Why take the lazy way out and call various companies that control or supply the workers rather than do it themselves and gain the added advantage of loyalty? Where do you stand?

The most powerful factor to your success is hiring the right people with the right attitude. It is more critical than knowledge!

Notes or Action Plans:

_____

_____

_____

_____

_____

_____

THE ENEMY OF CHANGE
IS COMPLACENCY

The changing of any position, procedure, or strategy is very difficult. As a progressive leader, you must address it objectively and not be lulled into complacency by either your employees or temporary success. Let me share some danger signals for successful leaders:

1. People do not really want to change what they are doing today.

2. Short-term gains from successful performance in the past allows the company to reason, "We are doing okay; we do not need any real change."

3. We will change, but let's do it slowly.

4. Management either doesn't want to take a risk, or (with staff influence) wants to proceed slowly (if at all).

5. Management decides that they will band-aid the situation until they are promoted and let someone else take the real risk of making change.

6. People feel that they are doing things as best as can be done. "It is the other guy causing the problems."

The starting points of change for successful leaders:

1. You recognize that you cannot survive by just doing more of what you are doing today.

2. You must reinvent the way you look at your business and how you handle it.

3. You must provide the vision and leadership to your people, and they must be empowered to assist you in achieving it. You alone must be the author of the vision with inputs from others. You must stand tall, take that first decisive

step, and maintain the discipline and patience to let your team learn these new skills.

4.   Once you have done the above, you should set a business plan that stretches out only eighteen months with very ambitious objectives that you can accomplish in a timely manner.

Communication is critical

Once your plan is developed, it is critical that you inform everyone as soon as possible so they can begin to buy into your plan, and to avoid rumors.

If you have a union, be sure to *bring your union leaders into your office* and share with them confidential data so they understand why it is critical that they cooperate. They must understand that making a profit is not a dirty word. Without profit, it is just a matter of time before something happens—you either go out of business or change your location. Either one will affect everyone in the present work force. They should all have a piece of the action to help push change, not resist it.

In any realistic plan, there will be a reduction of labor force; if not, it is not a realistic one. The right way to do it is to try to have everyone realize that no one will be released as a direct result of improving processes and productivity. As soon as you recognize who can be pulled off line, put those workers on special assignments, doing work that needs to be done immediately. This way, the product cost represents the *real* product cost and allows marketing and salespeople to go out and generate additional sales. Additional sales will require additional people, so they will be absorbed that way. Also, all new hires will be frozen, and you will let attrition help remove excess people and reduce the special projects accordingly.

Seasonal adjustments have been taking place for years in most businesses. It will continue to be based on seniority as it has been in the past. However, all special projects should then be reviewed to see if they are really needed. The continual practice of becoming more competitive may warrant some of the special projects being re-started. It is important that management evaluate these special projects *before* they start the process to ensure that they are value-added. (If you can't measure it, don't do it!)

Everyone, both salary and hourly, will be involved in the plan and in its implementation. Everyone must receive some type of reward and recognition as success is made. There may be such things as free pizza, tickets, fishing rods, dinners, or whatever suits the culture of your area. However, recognition must be made starting with employees achieving the task assigned. They can increase in value, such as an opportunity to develop technical skills at a local college. The company might also pay their entire wages while they are there for a certain time. Use your imagination, but do something now!

Notes or Action Plans:

_____

_____

_____

_____

_____

_____

_____

_____

_____

_____

_____

_____

_____

_____

_____

_____

_____

_____

_____

_____

_____

_____

_____

_____

_____

_____

_____

_____

_____

WITHOUT TRAINING
AND ACCOUNTABILITY,
EMPOWERMENT IS CHAOS

The latest rage that is taking place in the U.S. is to empower all employees. This is a very practical, sensible thing to do, particularly when, in many cases, they know the answer to the problems before you do. Why not have these highly skilled individuals assist you in solving these problems? All employees have a need for advancement, recognition, and security.

The problem, many times in our country, is that people are given too much empowerment too quickly. In doing so, things are not done in a timely manner because they have not been trained properly.

The management team cannot forsake their responsibility to manage and lead. Based upon their education, experience, and knowledge, they must determine the course that is needed not only to survive but also to prosper. They have the inputs from customers, the marketplace, the economy, periodicals and seminars, so they are strengthened and better trained to make the large decisions for what is needed for the business—they must perform this function.

In my visits to Japan, I observed that Japanese organizations that are making money run the business as if they were a military unit. The commanders do make the overall strategies, then the troops in the factories work as teams to help start the implementation and put into effect the decisions. It is not a democracy, and it should not be in the U.S. manufacturing if businesses want to compete world-wide; after all, if you continue that practice (and there are many doing it today), the inevitable will be that you will be out of business. World competition takes no prisoners.

Last thoughts in this area, I have seen CEOs and presidents delegating decisions to their staff about what needs to be done and how. There is a danger in giving too much delegation to your staff, in that you might not know what is going on until it is too late. Therefore, my suggestion is empower and delegate to them to decide what should be done, but the leaders should receive your final approval before taking action.

This gives you a chance to coach them if a decision or plan is something with which you feel uncomfortable. You can resolve it together before the action is taken. In the final analysis, as president or CEO, you are accountable, and you must advise them before making the final decision, rather than to blame them and have to take corrective action. This sounds simple, but you must coach without interfering, and sometimes this is difficult.

A secret danger for the president or CEO is being too patient and not wanting to upset staff members; you must always be in command or you are not needed.

Notes or Action Plans:

_____
_____
_____
_____
_____
_____
_____
_____
_____
_____
_____
_____
_____
_____
_____
_____
_____
_____
_____
_____
_____
_____
_____

KNOW THY ENEMY

It is interesting how many companies operate today in the marketplace, competing locally, domestically or globally without taking time to learn how they compare to the competition.

Companies will compare pricing because nothing happens in the marketplace until they decide at what price they are going to sell their product. They will try to figure what the going price is and what they can afford to sell it for, and then adjust; but, they will not take the time they should to study the enemy.

Business is war. To blindly go into battle, not knowing your enemy, is very foolish. It is the same in business.

For strategies, product planning, or advertising, you should always have at least one person as a designated opponent and a devil's advocate. The question is, "How will the competition react?"

In colleges or universities, athletic teams utilize scout squads that mimic the opponent's strengths. In your larger companies or corporations, there should be a designated group of people evaluating the competition. They should know what their opponents are doing. They should discover their strengths and weaknesses and exploit those, using strategic marketing plans.

There should never be a new product introduction without obtaining the best in the competition as a comparison to your prototype. Your prototype should project beyond that competitor's unit, because as you put yours to marketplace, they will be ready to improve theirs. You must leapfrog your competition so that they must follow you into the marketplace. This is a very critical thing to do, but it is amazing that most companies do not do it. The question is, "Do you?"

There are many ways to obtain intelligence about the competition. Let me list just a few:

1. Read the local newspaper—looking for the competition.

2. Search the Internet.

3. When interviewing a prospective new hire, debrief the candidate in detail for information.

4. Visit open houses held by other companies (as a tourist) to observe first-hand, the physical capabilities of their factories.

5. Read your competitors' advertising and literature. It will list their strengths, and you can play against them with your salespeople.

6. Association meetings attended by your competitors are great places to gather information. In addition, executives sometimes brag at bars or informal gathering places about their accomplishments or plans for the future. You can then offer this feedback to a central source at your facility.

7. Talk to your customers who have direct communication with the competition and ask what they think about your product versus your competition's product. Solicit feedback from them. Businesses often overlook this simple method of gathering intelligence.

8. Organize focus group meetings: bring in customers or various people off the street and talk about your product versus your competition's product. They might offer a clue that will enable your company to set itself over the competition.

If you do not have a designated "collector of intelligence" on your competition, you should form one immediately. It could be a small department or an individual. Employees carrying out this task will potentially save you their salary many times over, and save you from embarrassment in the marketplace.

In closing, it is critical that you are not blindsided or embarrassed because of your lack of attention to "know the enemy." To be forewarned is to be forearmed.

Notes or Action Plans:

_____

_____

_____

_____

_____

_____

_____

_____

_____

FORECASTING AND SCHEDULING ARE THE MAPS TO MAKING MONEY.

ARE YOU LOST?

If you talk to people in any kind of business that requires a forecast, they will tell you that it is extremely difficult to predict a forecast with any accuracy. Business requires an overall forecast for business planning; **but not for scheduling your manufacturing.**

If you talk to the people in the trenches in the organizations, they will tell you that they believe their building forecasts are the cause of some of their problems. This is because forecasts result in reactions instead of actions. They can cause surprise, corrections up or down and cause total chaos that costs hundreds of thousands of dollars annually.

Forecasting is like the weather in that everyone talks about it, but no one seems to be able to fix it. In the case of forecasting, when they can do something about it, they do not. Management often does this distasteful task at the very last minute before a meeting takes place, or passes it on to secondary people. Therefore, forecasting becomes an inaccurate road map for production.

For long-range planning, the real key is to attack *only the lead-times* in your facility. If you can minimize the amount of lead-time you require, then your delivery will be much shorter lead times. Having a shorter horizon will achieve more accuracy. It is also a cliché that if many people cannot forecast thirty days from now, they would not be able to forecast six months to a year from now. It is because it is handled poorly rather than professionally.

The people doing the scheduling should be your top, elite people. They should have a reservoir of information coming from trade magazines, their dealers, distributors, or customers. They should get clear information, such as government statistics and information gathered from talking to their customers, and present it in a meaningful way to track and adjust the forecast. A forecast is a map that does require adjustments, and it must be dynamic enough to reflect the changing conditions in the marketplace without being out of control, changing things haphazardly, or causing chaos. Forecasts must not only be in the manufacturing factories themselves, but also within suppliers who support the manufacturing plans or that company or corporation.

The way to look at forecasts overall, as I said earlier, is to reduce the lead-times but then forecast only what you must forecast. In other words, if you know that there are certain basic products you do not want to deplete, you should have the in-process inventory protected to allow for a sharp up-curve. Additionally, you need the discipline to watch it so that you do not go out of control with the inventory supplying it. Check the inventory forecast on a weekly basis to project accurately the lead-time required. Reduction of lead-time itself should be not only in the factory but also with the suppliers. If the whole system reduces its lead-time, then the accuracy is enhanced greatly, the confusion is reduced, and the customers are better served. The finished goods inventory should be held down to as low a level as possible, with the exception of built-to-order products. I suspect there are a few companies and corporations doing this today, but this will be the wave of the future.

The items that are the standard (or the stars of your product line) that you do not wish to be out of, should be handled with a version of "kanban," so that they are replenished quickly without losing control. A kanban, as you may know, is a replenishing system using indicators to make production systems respond to actual needs and not predictions or forecasts. The standard items are supported by a backup of in-process inventory to take care of seasonal spurts, but you should reduce or eliminate inventory in the off-season.

There may be certain items that you have in your product line that are very special. You should advertise to your customers that those require additional lead-time, and produced them on a build-to-order basis. If you do these two things, then the difference in the remaining items are the ones that you have to address strategically as to how you forecast them.

Therefore, forecasting for material should not be improved—it should be eliminated. The proper use of real-time kanbans builds in the safety and flexibility of seasonal changes, and reacts quickly to customer needs if done properly.

Notes or Action Plans:

_____

_____

_____

_____

_____

_____

_____

_____

_____

_____

_____

_____

_____

_____

_____

_____

_____

_____

_____

_____

_____

_____

_____

_____

_____

_____

_____

_____

_____

_____

_____

_____

_____

MEETINGS ARE THE RIFLES OF BUSINESS AND BULLETS ARE THE RESULTS.

ARE YOU SHOOTING BLANKS?

Many companies and corporations are overwhelmed with meetings. Meetings are important to communicate quickly on changing conditions or problems; but too often, meetings become either a habit or an excuse for not taking action.

In your organization, how much time do you spend in meetings? How much time do *your people* spend in meetings? How many meetings do you routinely schedule daily, weekly, and monthly? Do these meetings have benefit? If you don't have this information, get it now!

No one in management would suggest that meetings are unnecessary, but they do tie up valuable people. Put a dollar value on the time spent in a meeting and ask, "How much money have we saved?" You will find that many meetings held to resolve a problem are an ineffective waste of time because they are unnecessary or improperly planned.

Management often does not recognize one of the hidden costs of meetings. That is, customers cannot communicate with you or your key people when you are in meetings.

In a very aggressive marketplace, timely action is required to resolve immediate needs. When people are tied up in meetings, business and enthusiasm are lost, due to the lack of *action*. More often than not, customer calls are not returned in a timely fashion because personnel have so many meetings and phone calls. In addition, subordinates who need guidance or signatures are less than productive while waiting for supervisors to come out of meetings.

Using these simple criteria, you should make an evaluation for supervisor meetings:

1.   In all cases, decide if the meetings are value-added or non-value-added.

2.   Are the right people attending the meetings?

3.   Is there a time limit on meetings? Most meetings should not last longer than two hours. If they do, the agenda was improperly planned, the people were ill prepared, or you are overloading the people in the meeting. The results are far from favorable.

4.   Review the meetings being held and try to cancel as many as possible. Meetings should have a specific time limit and people should know ahead of time what is required of them so they can come prepared. You should cancel the meeting if people come to the meeting unprepared. Rescheduling it for after-hours will put peer pressure on those who were not ready.

Let me emphasize that rapid communication is required in the combat of business today. Do not use meetings as hideouts to avoid reality or as political places. If you do not address meetings properly, the true costs will be enormous. You should list all of the pitfalls that you are experiencing today. And, guess what? The money saved here will be significant, and it will not cost you one cent. What better advertising for your customers is there, than being able to talk to someone when they have a need?

If nothing else, empower certain people to make decisions or to answer customers' questions immediately. This way, a customer is seldom help up for answers!

Notes or Action Plans:

_____

_____

_____

_____

_____

_____

_____

PRODUCT LINE PROLIFERATIONS ARE LIKE BARNACLES ON A SHIP

It is amazing that nine out of ten people in an organization will tell you that they are against product proliferation—yet most organizations have products in their catalogs on which they do not make money. This can cause a real problem with product positioning because they overlap.

Also, in the field, workers are confused and frustrated that they have to carry so many part numbers for servicing products with low volume. In the factories, management never does figure the costs correctly, as they try to make obsolete parts for slow moving products.

These forgotten products (still in the catalogs) are costing you money to maintain the literature and the catalog space; but most importantly, it is costing you money to maintain the design. As things change, you have to update these designs as you try to standardize the components—even though they are built in very small quantities or not at all.

One easy-to-do analysis can either be done physically or by computer. The physical illustration is more of a dramatic gesture for the staff or your organization. What I have seen done is the general manager or the marketing people list all the products on a butcher-type paper (found in meat markets), and they put them on the wall of the conference room like a gallery of pictures. First, they list what the product is and the part number, then they list what the volume has been for the past two years separately, and then they list what the contribution to profit has been the last two years. The results show the volume in descending order and prompt the questions, "Why do we have this in the line? Will something else take its place? If not, what can be done to change designs so they are acceptable to the customer and still not a proliferation of product?"

Of course, a far easier way to do this is to program the computer and have it printed out in the spreadsheet format that you prefer, but either way is fine for big or small companies. The bottom line is that you want to see how many products that you build, what the volume of those products is, and what the profits are on those products or the margins being generated Then you can begin to prune your catalog or product line.

When a new model is about to be introduced, companies should consider when and how to phase-out older versions or models. There is an astounding amount of money thrown away by big and small companies on the introduction of new products. It is pretty basic that the new product should not be sent to the field until all old inventories has been exhausted, regardless of the screaming in the sales department to push the new product.

The experienced customer will wait until you discount these because now they are the old models. Unfortunately, sometimes these units are given away at a ridiculously low prices (or scrapped), thus robbing companies of any profit because of poor planning or introduction.

A company or corporation that has specialized, moneymaking products should not just cancel them. They should increase the price to the customer until they see the benefits of upgrading to the new model. Sometimes, as with children, you cannot give customers too many choices without spoiling them. The key is to satisfy customers' individual needs, while creating useful products that sell. Companies are in business to make money.

Most companies would benefit from some spring "housecleaning" on their products, service parts, and procedures to keep them current. When they do address this, they will be more flexible, react faster to the market, and make more profit.

What is your status? Do you have a plan?

Notes or Action Plans:

_____

_____

_____

_____

_____

_____

_____

_____

_____

_____

_____

CHANGE DESIGN EVERY YEAR, AND THE PLATFORM OF DESIGN EVERY THREE YEARS

You might have the best product in today's market, but six months from now, you might be in third or fourth place because of the tremendous speed with which new products and new technologies are introduced. Therefore, you must be careful that you do not become obsolete or an also-ran. At the same time, you must make money, so you cannot simply continue to spend capital and never get to the point of harvesting the large investments that you have made for your company or corporation.

One of the problems in designing a product is that, in order to be competitive and obtain the needed margins, the marketing department gives a target cost to the engineering department. In the process of design, and the pressure to meet or beat targets, designers begin to optimize their capabilities by reducing the costs on individual items by fractions or pennies. They then sometimes sub-optimize their design. For example, they may shorten the length of a lead wire or may use a substitute bolt, nut, screw, or fastener. If designers use their special fastener, they can save a few pennies on their particular design. They end up with a design that has special components rather than standardized components.

Management must begin to recognize this and hold the engineering department accountable for stabilizing the number of components in a given product. They should use as much standardization as they can when manufacturing the product, and satisfy the market with a unique product that calls for the margin for which you are planning on.

The engineering department can accomplish this with good discipline. Once the engineering department has its act together, they should be able to design the interior products so that the standard components will be as cross functional as possible. They should be able to simplify the design as much as possible so that the platform (the basic design) can be tooled and flexible to change over the next three years. This way, the capital costs can be harvested.

The trick is to have the envelope, or the cover of the product that the consumer sees, changed yearly. It can change color or decals, it can have minor tooling changes to it, or it can be changed by adding unique features to it every year so that it is special, different, and more acceptable to the consumer than it was the previous year.

This means that when individual components have been designated as acceptable (the best quality possible), the design itself should be flexible, so that a given platform can have variations to the exterior without affecting the main capital costs. The product can be introduced quickly, there will be product differential, and it will not be stagnant.

The platform design should be reviewed and altered every three to five years. Again, I stress that the platform design is not just that year's new design. It should be tooled without having to start from scratch, with the flexibility to change, without losing the capital tooling, and reducing the long lead-time of its introduction.

The design of the present and the future must begin to be simplified more. Products must be made simply, with the highest quality and flexibility, and by asking: "How can we better serve our customers? How can we give them, if you will, a better mousetrap than what is being used today rather than the same type of generic unit or product with a different dress on it?" In other words, look at the function and use of the product and see how you can add to its capabilities in ways that you never have—ways that will better serve your customers.

Remember, your product must meet have a "sizzle to it"—something real special.

Notes or Action Plans:

_____

_____

_____

_____

_____

_____

_____

_____

_____

TIME IS MONEY:

HOW ARE YOU SPENDING YOURS?

Time is irreplaceable. Regardless of your station in life, if you are poor or rich, there is one thing that is equal—there are only twenty-four hours in the day. One exciting part of life is that each and every person has the freedom of choice regarding how to use those twenty-four hours each day.

One of the universal problems is that most of us do not use it properly. Most of us become creatures of habit and go through a ritual through the better part of our day, predictably doing the same things at the same times over and over again. This also is true not only in our personal life, but also in our lives as executives and business people.

If you are not careful, you will fall into a standard routine, and you will go through this not recognizing that many of the variable conditions have changed around you in world competition and even in the health of your company or corporation. You must be on guard at all times to break the habit of repeatability and predictability. Challenge yourself to do different things, check new ways to operate and listen to new people, not the same few on a daily basis. Project yourself beyond where you are today with your customers, for example, and beyond that into your customers' customers, in focus groups and meetings.

If you do not do this, you become a prisoner—a prisoner of your mind, and your habits and values remain the same. On the other hand, if you give yourself a pardon and freedom from your prison, go out and meet new people, meet the customers' customers and get involved with details, you will refresh yourself and become more valuable. Your judgments will be much more effective and the company or corporation will profit much more than they are today. You will also have new youth, vigor, and energy to carry out your responsibilities.

Time is a great leveling field, but time can be your ally if you use it more wisely than your competition. It is time for you to sit back in a quiet place and evaluate what you do and when you do it on a daily basis. Ask yourself if you are building a wall around flexibility. If so, break through that wall and come out a new individual. Good luck and good hunting.

Notes or Action Plans:

_____

_____

_____

_____

_____

_____

_____

_____

_____

_____

_____

_____

_____

_____

_____

_____

_____

_____

_____

_____

_____

_____

_____

_____

_____

_____

_____

_____

THE RIGHT
MEASUREMENTS
ARE LIKE LIGHTHOUSES—
KEEPING YOUR SHIP
OFF THE ROCKS

The problem with industry today is measurement. Leaders often look for a silver bullet that will solve all problems of measuring. They retain old methods of measurement along with new ones, even though many of those methods have become obsolete.

The classic one that comes to my mind is the use of plant absorption. A surprising number of companies and corporations in the United States are still using the plant absorption measurement. It is obsolete because it is a direct enemy of cash flow. You artificially inflate your inventories to show labor absorption, and by doing so, you cause a need for more storage, which is cost; you cause a need for more fork-trucks, which is cost; you cause a need for more handling and record keeping, which is cost; and then there is not any time to recoup. Every month you need the absorption, so you continually carry this inventory, which is dollars, and some of it becomes damaged in its handling. In effect, like a drug once taken, it is difficult for many companies and corporations to stop. The answer, like drugs, is to say "no" to plant absorption and move into the real, modern world. In following through with this example on absorption, the answer is to go to the lean production approach. You give customers what they need faster than any competition today, and you command more margins because you are giving something to them that they cannot find elsewhere.

No more than five types of measurement should fit for your company or corporation. The one I suggest strongly in manufacturing is *product cost*. The challenge of manufacturing should be that *the product cost should be going down every week*. The company leaders should be penalized for carrying inventories; and they should be penalized for using too much lead-time. They need to change their way of doing business.

Take inventory of the various measurements under your command. You will be surprised at how many there are and how much money they are costing you. Confusion will be reduced if concentration is on just a few that everyone understands. If you are diligent, you will be successful—more so than what you are today. The old adage, "People do what the boss checks," is certainly true regarding measurements and the *actions necessary* to have the boss look good.

Notes or Action Plans:

_____
_____
_____
_____
_____
_____
_____
_____
_____
_____
_____
_____
_____
_____
_____
_____
_____
_____
_____
_____
_____
_____
_____
_____
_____

DO MORE PERKS
FOR YOUR CUSTOMERS
MEAN MORE BUSINESS?

More perks (or rewards) for your customers may not mean more business. One problem is that your customers are, in many cases, buying parts from other suppliers who also offer incentives, so it gets to be assumed as a cost of doing business.

This assumption is not correct if you investigate it thoroughly. The trips or golf outings are nice, but when offered a realistic price—one that does not include these rewards, most customers would prefer to have the best price and decide what *they* want to do with the savings—whether to reinvest in price differences or create their own. In many cases, the benefits themselves become very nice incentives for the executives of the companies and their people, which again add to the cost of doing business.

My counsel would be to have two prices, so you will not have these perks. For those who want the perks, the price is "X" number of dollars. Those who do not want the perks pay a lower price. You may find that business actually increases because you are not refusing the customer the privilege of a reward; you are giving him an opportunity to save money. In the worst-case scenario, customers will continue to buy the needed amount only from their supplier who offers these perks. The vast majority of the business, however, will be negotiated with you, because you have the lowest prices (as well as good quality and delivery).

This does not mean you have to completely eliminate any social contact with your customers, because there is a definite need for them to be recognized and have their egos stroked. Opportunities for this include supplier-sponsored meetings and dinners (or annual affairs) where they hand out awards for achievements, and customers are given recognition in front of their spouses and their peers. This is much more meaningful, but it does not mean you cannot engage in occasional, one-on-one golf outings with individual distributors. Again, it is more like contact and communication than a perk. Company leaders should reappraise the value of lavish, almost out-of-hand conventions and trips versus the options.

Notes or Action Plans:

_____

_____

_____

_____

_____

_____

_____

_____

_____

_____

_____

_____

_____

_____

_____

_____

_____

_____

_____

_____

_____

_____

_____

_____

_____

_____

_____

_____

_____

_____

_____

DOES DOWNSIZING ALWAYS SAVE MONEY?

It is a myth to believe that downsizing automatically saves money. It is the manner in which you perform downsizing that is important.

The approach should be to look at the total organization, and where possible, realign and consolidate responsibilities so that fewer people are needed; remove all waste from the office and the factory. This may not be enough to amount to true *downsizing* and you must be careful not to overload managers, causing access problems for the people reporting to them.

Downsizing may require that you move your organization or factories to a new state. This can give you an exceptional amount of money to move into an area and create a payroll for its communities, particularly in hard-pressed areas. It also gives you a chance to change your culture, your processes and systems, and remove any non-value-added steps that you have today. In other words, you should not take unproductive people with you to a new facility. You will be able to have a clean start as you think through downsizing with regard to fringe benefit costs, salary structures, hourly structures, medical costs, retirement costs and starting rates.

You cannot just reduce salary headcounts and say you are downsizing; you may initially save money, but if you do not change your organization or procedures, the system begins to fail and people are recalled. Poorly done, downsizing can actually cause you to lose money and customers.

Notes or Action Plans:

_____

_____

_____

_____

_____

_____

YOU NEED
A STRATEGIC PLAN
AND A BUSINESS PLAN

Many companies do not have any real planning. They are a reactive model when fire fighting through various conditions that occur. At best, they are reactive enough to be called successful (when not losing money). They are not really taking time to determine what business they are in, nor how they should react in this business, based on all of the conditions present.

More and more companies and corporations do not have strategic plans that extend beyond three years. They are lucky if they have a business plan that extends beyond twelve months. There is a need to have a business plan based on the latest information, the market trends, the economy, and the competition. To make money, you should be capable of tracking your company or corporation in order to meet market requirements.

Strategic planning is not just good, but critical to have. Overall, you should look at the state of business and anticipated growth factors so you can measure cash flow and have credit available. You should be looking at the marketplace and the need to change or the need to update technology. You need to look at the resources required for the future, to train people, and to develop new marketing approaches or distribution. Allow the materials people to work with suppliers to make sure they have enough capacity to support growth, necessary tooling, and capital. Plan to meet the anticipated sales, increased market share, and shorter lead-times.

In conclusion, what you really need is an eighteen-month business plan and follow-through. You should also have a three to five-year strategic plan for cash flow planning and capacity planning. You need both to be successful; having neither can lead to disaster.

Notes or Action Plans:

_____
_____
_____
_____
_____
_____
_____
_____
_____
_____
_____
_____
_____
_____
_____
_____
_____
_____
_____
_____
_____
_____
_____
_____
_____
_____
_____
_____
_____
_____
_____
_____
_____

JUST-IN-CASE INVENTORY IS A COST YOU CANNOT AFFORD

The "Just-In-Case Inventory Syndrome" is alive and well in many companies. This means that inventory is manufactured or purchased *just in case* they have an increase in business, *just in case* they have a mechanical problem, or *just in case* they cannot supply the demand. At the onset, it looks like a reasonable alternative. The real world facts are that management is unable to determine what mix of inventory they should have. Inventory ties up cash flow; however, that is not the end of the story.

One reason that the inventories are piling up, in many cases, is that the executives are not enlightened enough to be addressing needs, problems and demand. The problem might be merely a case of trying to keep employees busy. A supervisor might be combining jobs to make a three-to-four-week supply of products, thus keeping his employees busy and making his job easier.

A general supervisor or superintendent might think that by having all of the material available he is going to save money by eliminating shortages, combining the runs, or reducing the amount of setups. What really happens is they run out of capacity because they are running these parts too far-out, and the machines will not cycle fast enough. They work overtime to build up even more unnecessary inventory. Doing this ties up space, increases costs, and seriously affects cash flow.

If management adopts the Toyota Manufacturing strategy, which is the elimination of all waste, it will save a tremendous amount of money on inventory carrying cost; thus requiring less labor, space, capacity, and time. The end result will be that you actually have fewer shortages and more flexibility.

The main problem is, (many times) management assumes their supervisors are making the right decisions and does not even monitor the real work being done in day-to-day operations.

Notes or Action Plans:

_____
_____
_____
_____
_____
_____
_____
_____
_____
_____
_____
_____
_____
_____
_____
_____
_____
_____
_____
_____
_____
_____
_____
_____
_____
_____
_____
_____
_____
_____
_____
_____
_____

TAKE ACTION WHEN YOU ARE IN TROUBLE!

"Overkill" works when you are in trouble in *every situation*. For example: If you are requiring salaried people to address problems, particularly during seasonal pickup, do not risk failure by having insufficient salaried people on the job. Consider bringing in temporary salaried people (experienced ones if possible) and then attack the problem with this increased work force. As soon as the problem is solved, remove the temporary employees and reassess the work force and, based on their skills, make needed reductions. To that end, you will solve the problem while simultaneously increasing the quality of your work force.

If there is a quality problem, do not hesitate—attack it with vigor! Do not be timid to ask for help, internally or externally, and attack the problem quickly. Gather the facts, examine the details, and work overtime. Do not be conservative—solve the problem! In the end, you will save money.

Using the two examples above, you must examine the situation. If you are in bad trouble or heading in that direction, address the problem before it deteriorates any further. You can go back and find out what *first went wrong* and correct it. You can then upgrade the salary workforce and systems so that it will not occur again. I repeat, bottom line: when you have a serious problem do not "band-aid" it—immediately make it the focus of your attention using the best resources possible. "Overkill" the problem before it is out of control. You will save big money in the long run—and perhaps customers, too.

Notes or Action Plans:

_____

_____

_____

_____

_____

_____

THE MYTH OF CONTROLLING SALARY HEADCOUNTS

It is truly amazing that there are so many corporations in the United States who require their plant managers (or presidents in many cases), to get corporate approval to add a single salary headcount.

These same people, plant managers and presidents, can hire excess hourly people. No one challenges them on spending millions of dollars for purchasing materials, yet they are unable to perform their responsibility to hire salaried employees because senior management over-manages them.

It makes you wonder if senior management knows that they are in business to make money. They are not meant to be an impediment to making money, and they do not have the knowledge of what is required at a given facility.

A plant manager or general manager should be able to handle an agreed-upon budget. If they fail, then proper discipline should be taken. Otherwise, it should be hands off.

If senior management has time to over-manage these small things such as individual headcounts, clerks and secretaries in facilities, you have to wonder what they are doing with their time. Are they are contributing to making money or are they, themselves, a non-value added individual?

Notes or Action Plans:

_____
_____
_____
_____
_____
_____
_____
_____

MAXIMUM REDUCTION
OF LAYERS OF
MANAGEMENT

A maximum reduction of layers of management should be examined with pride for many organizations, ideally concluding they have little bureaucracy between the hourly employees and top management. It is not healthy, though, to arbitrarily reduce the layers of management. Again, I remind you that the purpose of being in business is to make money, not to engage in politics.

In many organizations where layers of management have been removed, the structures have not changed the process. The only real thing that was accomplished beyond the paper savings is a lack of control and reduction in communication.

It is extremely difficult to work with an expanded staff and give them the necessary time they need for training and counsel. It is also difficult for individual people to make contact by phone with their superiors because they are tied up with other responsibilities. The result is that poor decisions are made, and consultation time is not used effectively. Morale is poor in the employee's area beneath the executives. Even the executive knows he is not covering the ground, as he should. Some of the casualties of this type of organization, besides pre-tax, are the executive's family time and the general morale of the organization.

The only way for an organization to take out layers of management is to restructure in a manner that allows empowerment in certain areas. You may not call them supervisors anymore, but they will be performing the same functions. In removing layers of management, other things to consider are combining departments and reassigning responsibilities. For example, business administration takes over the responsibilities and has the supervisors report to them in matters of accounting, data processing and developing human resources.

Too many times, the sad truth is that this is done to impress stockholders and top executives who do not want to be left behind because they read about the latest trends and recent changes in the industry. In summary, you cannot reduce the people or change an organization without changing the process you will encounter unacceptable risks.

Notes or Action Plans:

_____
_____
_____
_____
_____
_____
_____
_____
_____
_____
_____
_____
_____
_____
_____
_____
_____
_____
_____
_____
_____
_____
_____
_____
_____
_____
_____
_____
_____
_____

LEVEL LOADING IS A MYTH

One of the greatest myths of the last twenty years is that senior management believes they can solve their seasonality problems in the marketplace by level loading their factories.

They have also identified level loading as the way to avoid turnovers at the factories, please the unions, and have good morale by avoiding overtime and not having layoffs. These practices contribute to the myth that this can be done efficiently.

The traditional way of level loading the schedules has been to pre-build the inventory required in order to take off the peaks and put in the valleys. The danger in doing this is that there is a tremendous amount of dollars tied up inventory, and the hidden costs of this inventory are the warehousing, handling, scrap and the mix problems. You never have the correct mix on what you need—either too much or too little. There is a real danger of having obsolescence by pre-building.

Of course, another casualty is cash flow. Tying up all this money by using the magic tool of level loading has caused many companies and corporations serious trouble and survival difficulties. The average corporation goes through a "fire sale" of inventory when the profit is not there.

Management would be better off studying the alternatives to level loading. One alternative is to take the people they have in their facilities and make sure they are staffing the critical processes and bottlenecks in the factories. When the seasonal highs pick up and overtime is required, they can bring in a temporary workforce to work in the unskilled areas of a facility. The temporary employees would leave at the end of the season.

This is not easily done. It requires training money, cross training time and financial compensation for the permanent assignment of some people to more highly skilled positions. It is worth the extra money to have them. They should be owner-operators responsible for the quality and the minor maintenance as well as the productivity of their areas.

The human resources department has to be more creative in developing their own temporary workforce. College students, retirees, police officers, firefighters, and second-shift homemakers working four hours a day, often prove to be a quality workforce. This is the only way that you can really give the customer what they want, when they need it, without running the risk of having obsolete scrap and a cash flow problem. It takes the leadership that companies often lack.

The real objective is to develop a strategy to use a pull system (build-to-order), then a forecast system. One of the strategies needed is to maximize the critical processes for quality and flexibility. It may even require outsourcing parts *in-season* to supplement production and bring it back in the *off-season*.

Notes or Action Plans:

_____

_____

_____

_____

_____

_____

_____

_____

_____

_____

_____

_____

_____

_____

_____

_____

_____

_____

_____

_____

_____

_____

_____

_____

_____

_____

MISAPPLICATION
OF LEAN PRODUCTION
CAN BE DISASTROUS

I would like to caution you against using lean manufacturing incorrectly. Let me cite some examples.

You should never try to improve an obsolete strategy or process; therefore, I would suggest that before you implement lean manufacturing, you explore the possibility of outsourcing all but your core processes in season and the option to recall them in off-season if the price is right. Many small and medium sized suppliers might give you an advantageous break on pricing to get incremental volume increase on their core processes and capital utilization.

I am thinking of press parts, welded parts, plastic parts, sub-assemblies, and so forth, that can be delivered daily on large parts—or replenishing kanbans on smaller ones. In fact, with the right volume, they might lease a building close to your factory and even consider buying or leasing some of your excess equipment. The point being, you want to lower your total cost as much as possible; this may be better than to improve an outdated strategy of vertical integration using lean manufacturing.

We have seen companies or corporations install lean manufacturing in one area or department and for whatever reason, stop there. In a surprisingly short time, this lean manufacturing area is alien to the rest of the factory and begins to slip back to the old methods as much as it can.

In implementing lean manufacturing, you must agree that it is going to be a continuing process until the whole facility has been updated.

Another misapplication using lean manufacturing is the use of your own people to implement it. They are likely to do a very good job on the 5 S's but then fail to reduce the waste of too much labor. The reason for this is that these employees work in the same facility and they do not want to be thought of as the enemy for creating reductions of labor. We have seen this happen when a lean manufacturing return on investment was very disappointing. We believe that outside consultants in this case can serve a good purpose providing they guarantee a return of 200% of all their expenses. I suggest the correct way of reducing excess labor headcounts is to communicate properly with the work force the truth—that in order to be competitive against world competition, we must reduce our costs for job security.

I would then give all of them exposure in a short presentation about what lean manufacturing and Kaizen events really mean, what they can accomplish, and that the following reductions will take place:

1. You would immediately freeze hiring of all permanent headcounts and will use temporary people only if needed. The plan is to use attrition and retiree employees to reduce headcounts as much as possible.

2. During the process of implementation, any excess hourly people will be removed immediately (based on seniority) and put into a labor pool and used as replacements for attrition and retired employees.

3. Management will also look at buying a product from another corporation to absorb any excess hourly.

4. If management does not find a product to bring in right away or expand its product line and the labor pool grows, there may be seasonal layoffs (based on seniority).

Notes or Action Plans:

_____
_____
_____
_____
_____
_____
_____
_____
_____
_____
_____
_____
_____
_____
_____

PLANT ABSORPTION IS A FALSE CONCEPT

Factories have been measured on absorption for the past forty years. In other words, the measurement of manufacturing has been the amount of labor required of in-process inventory (converted to finished goods). Labor receives credit to manufacture it. In a sense, it has been their pre-tax.

Even today, it is amazing to see top executives call up plant managers to tell them they need more absorption and encourage them to produce more inventories that no one needs. This affects cash flow so that they can come up with a fictitious profit statement to media forecasts. These executives are obsolete and should be re-educated or dismissed.

The only true measurement for manufacturing should be product cost. One product cost that can be directly controlled is labor. Labor reduction should take place every week. Reduce the labor required of a product by using lean production, making engineering changes, or increasing efficiency using new technology. The key is to have labor reduced every single week.

In most cases, the material content carries more dollar than labor, and so this, too, should be examined. There must be a continued reduction of material costs by redesigning, reducing cost, or obtaining new suppliers. Therefore, in measuring a factory, you have the flexibility to address labor, material, or burden. Each of these should be going down every week, and if it does, it gives you an increase in margin. It also gives the marketing in top management the ability to create a war chest to reduce the price (if required) to increase share of market; thus generating more business.

The only measurements that should be used throughout the organization should be those that contribute to making money. Any other measurement that takes away the capability of making money should be eliminated. The objective is to have *value-add* at all times, not to create false inventory requirements.

Notes or Action Plans:

_____
_____
_____
_____
_____
_____
_____
_____
_____
_____
_____
_____
_____
_____
_____
_____
_____
_____
_____
_____
_____
_____
_____
_____
_____
_____
_____
_____
_____
_____
_____
_____
_____
_____
_____
_____

LONGER LEAD-TIMES ARE NOT BETTER; THEY ARE A DISASTER

Having longer lead-time is a false misconception in planning for your customers' orders or supplier lead-time. The novice approach is that the more lead-time you have, the better off you are.

Actually, the more lead-time you have, the more changes you have in the interim period because no one can forecast accurately what the customers will demand even thirty days out; trying to go sixty or ninety days tends to be futile.

Better planning is the answer to avoiding longer lead-time, thus reducing lead-time in the factory process. Most everything manufactured today by operation or by assembly, including cars, is done in less than four hours time, per cycle, per unit. Most items are a matter of a few minutes; therefore, to have supplier lead-time of eight to ten weeks is obsolete. You must work with suppliers (as well as your own factory processing), so you can cycle fast enough to reduce to as close to build-to-order as possible, particularly on the special items. On the standard items, you should have sufficient inventory forecast so that you can react quickly. The only controlling factor will be the cycle time. One way of using this type of safety stock is to use kanban inventory so that you can automatically reorder as needed. You maximize the amount of inventory investment you have, and then you can calculate and adjust your risks so that it suits your business and your financial ability.

One way to reduce chaos is to shorten your in-house lead-times to a matter of days (I suggest three days). Then, freeze it. Any changes in schedules can take place (using my suggestion) on the fourth day, and everything started in the system is completed on schedule. You will not be causing confusion by changing schedules in process. The pressure will be on purchasing material not in-house scheduling. This is a huge dollar savings.

Notes or Action Plans:

_____
_____
_____
_____
_____
_____
_____
_____
_____
_____
_____
_____
_____
_____
_____
_____
_____
_____
_____
_____
_____
_____
_____
_____
_____
_____
_____
_____
_____
_____
_____

REDUCTION OF SALARY BY A PERCENTAGE IS A DANGEROUS CONCEPT

Even though it should have been obsolete twenty to thirty years ago, it is still a practice to arbitrarily set an objective of, say, a ten percent reduction of all salary headcounts. The end result of an edict to reduce by a percentage leaves most managers looking at their lowest echelon of people—reducing the Indians and keeping the chiefs on board. Then, even though the headcount numbers are reduced, the salary reduction is not that significant in terms of dollars.

A better way of mandating, if you have to, is to look at salary headcounts dollar-wise and never ask for a percentage of headcount reductions. Say that you want a ten percent reduction in your salary dollar budget. This requires your managers to rethink their organization intelligently and decide from where the dollars will come. They will quickly see that they are better off taking out a few chiefs, because their chiefs' salaries are normally two to three times the Indians' salaries. So, with fewer chiefs, you can save a lot of Indians, and in the final analysis, it is the Indians who do most of the work rather than the chiefs. **Never give an edict to reduce a percentage of headcounts. It should always be a percentage of a dollars-budgeted salary.**

At the conclusion, make each manager tell you what he is doing differently to ensure the work is being completed properly and on time, so as not to fail your systems.

Notes or Action Plans:

_____
_____
_____
_____
_____
_____

JAPANESE *"JUST-IN-TIME"* INVENTORY MUST BE UNDERSTOOD

There has been a lot of literature written about the Japanese who have "Just-In-Time" (JIT) inventory delivered to their factories. If you visit a few of their factories (for instance, the automotive factories in the U.S.), you will find, however, that the Japanese have material delivered within hours of its need. In order to be a supplier, in most cases, you must have several days (if not weeks) of inventory in a bonded warehouse very close by so that there is a chance for flexibility in schedules.

Therefore, do not think that there is such a thing as a free lunch by just specifying that you want material delivered by a certain hour and no more than "X" number of hours of production.

You must sit down and plan with the suppliers what your needs are; and where possible, use consignment inventories which you do not pay for until you use. If you have a large enough volume, you can encourage your suppliers to use a satellite warehouse close by to give you the quick delivery the Japanese do not publicize but are doing this in their automotive factories. This will give you flexibility and just-in-time inventory, and it is not in your records until they ship it from the warehouse to your facility.

In the case of internal manufacturing, you can require (and should get) just-in-time delivery. All your departments should be working on large parts that flow per schedule into the assembly area whose schedules are being pulled by customers' demands. In small parts, they should be set up across the board on in-house kanban so you limit the size of runs into inventory based on your seasonality. In season, you would increase your kanbans, and out of season, you would decrease the kanbans so that you maintain a healthy internal cash flow.

In closing, just-in-time inventory is the result of a lot of hard work; consistency; and most importantly, a realistic assembly schedule to which you adhere. It should have a frozen schedule with changes being made only in extreme emergencies.

Notes or Action Plans:

_____
_____
_____
_____
_____
_____
_____
_____
_____
_____
_____
_____
_____
_____
_____
_____
_____
_____
_____
_____
_____
_____
_____
_____
_____
_____
_____
_____
_____
_____

CAREFUL!
MISS AN OBJECTIVE AND
YOU ARE CHASTISED.
MISS DOING WHAT IS
"POLITICALLY CORRECT"
AND YOUR CAREER IS
SCARRED FOR LIFE!

In many cases, this saying is an unspoken truth in business. You can be performing in an excellent fashion, but have your career scarred, if not totally destroyed, by doing something that is being perceived as politically incorrect by higher management.

This poorly kept secret could be the result of your best intentions. Contrary to what is sometimes said, management does not always want you to tell them the real truth. They do not really want you to disagree with them, nor do they want you to steal their limelight by receiving public notice on accomplishments you have made.

Therefore, tread lightly, learn the unwritten rules of your culture, and maintain control of your ego. Use a healthy dose of common sense. This secret was saved for last, and few people will say it exists in their organization publicly; but perhaps it is the biggest secret I can share with you. It is alive and well in all business and social organizations today.

This disease in our country is causing the loss of excellent suggestions—and waiting to see what the boss wants to hear too often results in bad decision-making. It is costing your company or corporation millions of dollars a year. You must destroy this disease now by making sure you "don't shoot the messenger," even if they are presenting something that you perceive as politically incorrect.

You must encourage everyone's thoughts and ideas. Then, you take the expert and make a decision about what you want to do—because the buck stops with you in the final analysis. I also think you should share with those who gave input why you decided what you did and make an effort to publicly recognize the workers who gave valuable inputs.

Notes or Action Plans:

_____

_____

_____

_____

_____

_____

_____

_____

_____

_____

_____

_____

_____

_____

_____

_____

_____

_____

_____

_____

_____

_____

_____

_____

_____

_____

_____

_____

"LAST BUT NOT LEAST"

TWO POINTS THAT CAN MAKE THE DIFFERENCE IN YOUR SUCCESS

1. Most executives know about the 20/80 rule: 20% of all business, cost, etc. normally equals 80% of the total—right? However, in most daily functions or activities, they give equal value to the entire 100%. ***How do you operate?***

2. It is not *planning* that makes a business successful; it is ***timely implementation*** and changing tactics when needed! Be flexible and persistent to win and you will!

HOW DO YOU SCORE ON THESE?

Notes or Action Plans:

_____
_____
_____
_____
_____
_____
_____
_____
_____
_____

SUMMARY

1. In business, it isn't necessarily what you read that is important, *it's what action you take as a result of what you read.*

2. Always ensure that timely action is taken with deliberate speed.

3. Remember, always over-react on problems quickly, rather than to lose control because you thought *it maybe would go away.*

    ### Good luck and good hunting!

THINGS TO PONDER

1. Business is war—only the believers will survive.

2. Reward the believers and remove the unbelievers quickly.

3. The ultimate of perfection is simplicity.

4. As China's economy explodes even more, they may force American companies out of China to use the factories for their needs.

5. How much time do you _really_ spend on designing your products?

6. Employees must earn your respect with performance before you become good friends. If you're very easy and understanding initially in a new management position, and things aren't going well, it will be more difficult to achieve results because your expectations were too low to begin with.

7. Always continue to reduce your in-house lead times to a matter of hours or days. You should then freeze this schedule to avoid chaos in changing what is in process in the factory to meet new needs. You then should use kanban strategies for purchased parts, in-house and at suppliers. Speed is a very powerful, competitive weapon.

8. If you're sloppy and loose in scheduling and controlling meetings, then you will normally be sloppy in handling your business decisions. Meetings should be results-oriented and crisp in their execution. If you do this, your whole business culture will have a sense of being results-oriented.

9. Consider the option of outsourcing newly designed manufactured parts until the volume warrants hard tooling cost and then brought in-house.

10. New designs must have a 25-40% reduction in material content. Accept nothing less.

11. New designs also must be changed to minimize the cost of capital equipment and designed so that they can be produced with a maximum of quality and productivity.

12. Question how much time do you have in a given day and how you plan to use it effectively. (Do you have a plan?)

13. Business is the trading of dollars. Make all your measurements result in terms of dollars used—a powerful change to your culture

14. Sales thoughts: Many customers do not like their suppliers buying doughnuts or going to golf because it's taking up their people's time, but they are hesitant to tell their suppliers' management because it might offend them and affect their pricing. How does your team operate?

15. A poorly understood and seldom used tool (unbelievable but true) is called process mapping. This tool is powerful in evaluating the manufacturing processes to determine areas to reduce waste of time and effort. But, it is equally powerful in the salary function, which, in many cases, has savings greater than you would find in manufacturing (savings, fewer salary headcounts, less duplication, faster time and more flexibility).

16. A shocking fact: 90% of all top executives fail to take timely action when needed. What is your team's batting average? One example in industry is the inefficient way new product introductions take place.

17. Effective training or retraining is the cheapest, effective tool management has to be successful. How does your training measure up? The savings is beyond productivity; you will find that your employees are more enthusiastic and it becomes a morale booster as well. One advantage of training is that you will be able to quickly sort out the people who are trainable or expendable.

18. Discipline for success: Key information must be made available in a timely and accurate manner to be effective. Anything less is unacceptable.

EPILOGUE

If you found at least one idea that is worth exploring in this book, your time was not wasted. Our organization, World Competition Consultants, was founded in 1993. Prior to that, I was a former president of Carrier Canada. I was then president of their largest division, Residential Heating and Cooling ($1 billion in sales annually).

In starting our consulting business, my major tenant is that we will take all the risk, not our clients. That was what I experienced in my business life.

I would like WCC to be our clients' personal business doctor. Our objective is to earn the confidence and trust of our clients, just as they have in their family doctors. We will be there when needed, 24 hours a day, 7 days a week. (We do make house calls.)

We have thirty-five proven specialists who collectively can address all the disciplines or problems in engineering, marketing, manufacturing, sales or distribution. Our specialty is closing and moving factories.

I would like to consider WCC as an imaginary business hospital that will address our clients' special needs quickly and successfully whenever it is needed.

I urge you to consider us on a special offer. We will come into your facility, make a complete audit of your entire factory, and report our findings to you and your staff. We will not charge you anything for our time. Your only cost will be for our traveling expenses. We always try to leave at least one idea that you can implement quickly that will more than pay for our expenses. So, you then have a chance to get an outside set of eyes give you a thorough evaluation of what you are doing well and what you are doing better. This is at no risk or obligation and little if any cost.

Why not call us now? I welcome any comments, suggestions, or questions you might have.

Call me directly.

Roger G. Lewandowski, CEO
World Competition Consultants
(865) 681-3844

Roger@wcconsultants.com
WCConsultants.com
Cell: (865) 414-9009

Special note: Mr. Roger G. Lewandowski is available as a speaker or personal coach.

Specialists in rapid implementation

World Competition Consultants
"Eight Office Wastes"

1. Obsolete job descriptions

2. Obsolete processes being used

3. Duplications

4. Average Productivity in an office force is 55%

5. Too many chiefs

6. Lack of trained supervisors

7. Lack of motivation

8. Very slow and not flexible

Let us work with your team to address this "sleeping" opportunity for big savings and better service to your customers, both internally and externally.

Roger Lewandowski, CEO
World Competition Consultants
(865) 681-3844
www.wcconsultants.com

Specialists in rapid implementation

THE DEADLY SINS OF BUSINESS

1. "It is not that management does not know what to do or that they are in trouble, but it is their failure to take timely action that creates crisis."

2. "Trying to make an obsolete process or strategy effective and not recognizing the situation as it is."

3. "The dynamics of the world's marketplace is changing constantly. It is no longer acceptable to just be good at what you do, because in today's world, you might be doing the wrong thing."

4. "The single most common failure in management is failure to manage the implementation of plans quickly."

5. "Amazingly, the most overlooked marketing and sales tool is exceptional customer service in all that you do."

6. There is such a feeling of being "politically correct" that employees do not fully state their real opinion. This is causing a lot of valuable input to be "shut down."

7. Management does not think out of the box on the options of business competition as much as they should to compete with World competition.

Roger G. Lewandowski, CEO
World Competition Consultants
(865) 681-3844
www.wcconsultants.com

978-0-595-43425-1
0-595-43425-8

www.ingramcontent.com/pod-product-compliance
Lightning Source LLC
Chambersburg PA
CBHW030851180526
45163CB00004B/1536